Discovering Your Spiritual Gifts

J. E. O'Day

InterVarsity Press
P.O. Box 1400, Downers Grove, IL 60515-1426
World Wide Web: www.ivpress.com
E-mail: email@ivpress.com

InterVarsity Press® *is the book-publishing division of InterVarsity Christian Fellowship/USA*®*, a movement of students and faculty active on campus at hundreds of universities, colleges and schools of nursing in the United States of America, and a member movement of the International Fellowship of Evangelical Students. For information about local and regional activities, write Public Relations Dept., InterVarsity Christian Fellowship/USA, 6400 Schroeder Rd., P.O. Box 7895, Madison, WI 53707-7895, or visit the IVCF website at <www.intervarsity.org>.*

All Scripture quotations, unless otherwise indicated, are taken from the Holy Bible, New International Version®. NIV®. *Copyright* ©1973, 1978, 1984 by International Bible Society. Used by permission of Zondervan Publishing House. All rights reserved.

ISBN 978-0-87784-071-8

Printed in the United States of America ∞

P	31	30	29	28	27	26	25	24	23
Y	23	22	21	20	19	18	17		

Jesus said, "Even the Son of Man did not come to be served, but to serve, and to give his life as a ransom for many" (Mk 10:45). Since Jesus gave his life to serve others, we ought also to devote ourselves to the same thing. This is the purpose of Christ's calling: "We have been released from the law so that we *serve* in the new way of the Spirit" (Rom 7:6).[1]

In order to serve others, Jesus has given his people spiritual gifts. Yet Christians sometimes fall short in actually using their gifts. Many are standing on first base when instead they need to be running the base paths. One reason for this situation is they are unaware of their spiritual gifts.

For a number of years I did not realize I had the

gift of organization. My not knowing, however, did not keep me from using this gift. It did not prevent me, for instance, from organizing a strategy for our Inter-Varsity chapter during my college years. But now, aware that organization is one of my spiritual gifts, I consciously make choices and take paths which put my gift to work. When asked to chair my church's governing board, for example, I did not hesitate to accept. But here is the problem for many Christians. How can you know what gifts you have?

Defining Spiritual Gifts

Theologians have provided ample definitions of what the Bible means by the term *spiritual gift*. But Peter gives us a simple, practical handle on it when he writes, "Each one should use whatever gift he has received to serve others, faithfully administering God's grace in its various forms" (1 Pet 4:10). That is, a spiritual gift is *God's grace manifested in specific service to others.*

God's grace is made apparent to other people when we serve them in a concrete way. Every time we use our spiritual gifts, we are ministering God's grace to others—we are making God's grace visible to those around us. God's grace, his enabling power, makes us able to serve.[2] So a spiritual gift is *God's enabling power made visible by means of a particular type of activity which serves other people.*

Moreover, we find in 1 Peter 4:10 that grace has "various forms." Although all grace is the same enabling power of God, it enables different people in different ways. Grace is varied for two reasons: first, each person is unique and, second, there is a diversity of spiritual gifts. As the apostle Paul says in Romans 12:6, "we have different gifts, according to the grace given us."[3]

In 1 Peter 4:10 and Romans 12:6 we see a close relationship between gift and grace. First of all, gifts correspond to the particular grace we have received. Second, the relationship seems to be one of cause and effect. Our spiritual gifts differ because God's grace to each of us is different. We find diversity in spiritual gifts because God's grace bears such a rich diversity. God's gifts are inseparable from his grace, for grace is their source.[4]

Such an understanding of spiritual gifts leads us to two conclusions. (1) Every person who has received grace has already received spiritual gifts. (2) Every Christian has the responsibility to use his or her spiritual gifts in serving others. As Jesus' followers we are to employ God's gifts to serve. Jesus set the example and God has given us the ability. How can we do otherwise?

Discovering Your Gifts

If all of this is true, then it certainly follows that we ought to learn *what* spiritual gifts God has chosen to bestow on us. One of our spiritual goals should be to discover the gifts that came with God's grace. This is not an ethical duty: there is no such scriptural command. But it is the wise and expedient thing to do. And, as we have seen from 1 Peter 4:10, it *is* our ethical duty to *use* the gifts that God has given us. This command implies a prior knowledge of those gifts. It isn't that we can't serve without a conscious awareness of our gifts. As a matter of fact, most Christians are already using their spiritual gifts to one degree or another, even though they haven't identified them. But they could use them more effectively, more frequently, more decisively and more strategically if they became consciously aware of what spiritual gifts they possessed. In other words, a better knowledge of our gifts will help us serve others better.

Spiritual gifts are like words. In our everyday conversation we use thousands of words. But if in the course of a conversation someone suddenly asked us to define a certain word we had just used, we might be hard pressed to do so. But the amazing thing is that we *do* use words we can't define, and we usually use them *correctly*.

This is how it is with spiritual gifts. When we become Christians, we receive grace. This grace enables us to serve others in specific ways that correspond with the grace we have received, with the way that God has made and is remaking us. If someone were suddenly to ask us what gifts we possess, we might perhaps stare blankly. But meanwhile we have been using our unknown gifts.

When we know the definition of a word, we can use it with greater variety, more frequency, more accuracy and greater skill than when we do not. The same is true about spiritual gifts. Those who have identified their gifts use them more fully than those who have not.

Now you may be thinking, "This sounds all well and good, but how do I get from where I am to where I should be? What exactly should I look for to discover my spiritual gifts?"

Let's look first at what the Scriptures say.

The Scriptural Data
The New Testament identifies for us a great number

of specific spiritual gifts. The bulk of them are found in seven passages: Romans 12:6-8; 1 Corinthians 12:8-10, 28; 13:1-3; 14:26; Ephesians 4:11; and 1 Peter 4:11. My list of New Testament gifts numbers twenty-five:

1. Prophecy (Rom 12:6; 1 Cor 12:10, 28; 13:2; Eph 4:11)

2. Service/help (Rom 12:7; 1 Pet 4:11)

3. Ability to help (1 Cor 12:28)

4. Teaching (Rom 12:7; Eph 4:11; 1 Cor 12:28; 14:26)

5. Encouraging/comforting/urging/counseling (Rom 12:8)

6. Sharing/giving (Rom 12:8; 1 Cor 13:3)

7. Being a leader/managing/caring for (Rom 12:8)

8. Ability to lead/administration (1 Cor 12:28)

9. Being merciful/being kind (Rom 12:8)

10. Apostles (Eph 4:11; 1 Cor 12:28)

11. Evangelists (Eph 4:11)

12. Pastors (Eph 4:11)

13. A word of wisdom (1 Cor 12:8)

14. A word of knowledge (1 Cor 12:8; 13:2)

15. Faith (1 Cor 12:9; 13:2)

16. Healing (1 Cor 12:9, 28)

17. Workings of miracles (1 Cor 12:10, 28)

18. Ability to discriminate between spirits (1 Cor

12:10)
19. Tongues (1 Cor 12:10, 30; 13:1; 14:26)
20. Interpretation of tongues (1 Cor 12:10, 30; 14:26)
21. Speaking (1 Pet 4:11)
22. Celibacy (1 Cor 7:7)
23. Marriage (1 Cor 7:7)
24. Singing (1 Cor 14:26)
25. Revelation (1 Cor 14:26)

Consider carefully these gifts as you start out to discover your own. You will probably find that you possess one or more of them. But maybe not. Here is where confusion can set in. Don't be fooled into thinking that these are the only gifts God has given his people!

Virtually all theologians agree that the biblical lists of gifts are not exhaustive.[5] First, the Bible nowhere claims that the gifts listed by the apostles Paul and Peter are the only ones. Second, the seven lists are not identical. There are, in fact, considerable differences (for example, gifts that occur in only one list) and overlap (for example, prophecy and teaching), as a careful look at the references will confirm. If Paul knew that only a certain number of gifts existed, he likely would have called attention to that fact and made sure that all his lists agreed.

But they do not.

Third, we should not view the lists as exhaustive because the relationship between specific spiritual gifts and universal Christian responsibilities is unclear. Curiously, several of the gifts mentioned in the Bible are also characteristics which must be, or should be, the possession of all God's people. Faith, evangelism, giving, serving, encouraging and even teaching fall into this category. If this is true, perhaps the opposite is also true. It is probable that some Christians are specially gifted in one or more areas of universal Christian responsibility, such as hospitality, love, prayer, joyfulness and humility. This consideration would in itself expand the list of gifts considerably.

A fourth reason we should not limit ourselves to the biblical lists is the uncertain nature, or denotation, of many of the gifts mentioned. Christians disagree over the meanings of such gifts as *a word of wisdom, a word of knowledge, the ability to discriminate between spirits, healing,* and even *faith.* The reason for this is that the Scriptures just don't give us much information to go on. Paul does not elaborate on many of the gifts, so differences of opinion about what these terms refer to will always exist. Adding to this confusion is the fact that some of the gifts appear to be broad categories which comprise a number of gifts. For example, consider *teaching, evangelism, encouraging/comforting/urging/counseling* (all possible translations of the Greek word *parakalon*), *serving, being merciful* and *speaking*.[6] There are definitely several kinds of gifts within each of these categories, again expanding the list.

All these considerations make it difficult to be dogmatic about what is and what is not a spiritual gift. So don't be. Don't confine yourself to the gifts named in the Bible when you look for your own. Trying to squeeze your gifts into the mold of those listed in the New Testament could be very discouraging! Some of your gifts may be listed in Scripture, some may not. Let's not get caught up in a legalism that demands our gift be explicitly named in Scripture or that insists on our using the "correct" word or formulation. Let us rather get to work serving each other for the sake of the kingdom of Christ.[7]

Steps of Discovery
Notice that, in the list of twenty-five spiritual gifts, what might be called natural abilities are listed right beside some rather extraordinary gifts. Some spiritual gifts are, in fact, abilities that anyone might have, whether Christian or not. Many unbelievers

have gifts of leadership, teaching, singing, giving and hospitality. What makes the spiritual gift different? What makes it "spiritual"?

"If anyone is in Christ, he is a new creation; the old has gone, the new has come!" (2 Cor 5:17). When we become Christians, everything becomes new. And this includes natural abilities. Spiritual gifts often include natural abilities which God re-creates along with our whole being when he imparts grace to us and makes us new in Christ.

The God who created us with our particular and unique abilities, talents, inclinations and creativity is the same God who re-creates us from spiritually dead people to those who are alive to God through Christ Jesus. Our Creator is also our Redeemer. The Bible teaches that each of us is an integrated whole.[8] God is not going to violate this integrity when he regenerates us. He doesn't start from scratch but builds on what he's already made. As you begin the steps of discovery that follow, look for abilities you had as a non-Christian as well as for some new abilities God may have given you.

Prayer. Prayer is the first step. If you really mean business in your search, you will ask God to show you your gifts. God wants you to be aware of your gifts and will lead you in an exciting journey of discovery. If you are faithful in prayer, he promises to answer you (Mt 7:7-11). Make the discovery of your spiritual gifts the object of daily, persistent prayer. Praying is consistent with our profession of faith in an omnipotent yet immanent God.

Scripture. Step two is to study Scripture. I have already referred to several biblical passages. Look these up and study them for yourself. Become convinced of what the Scriptures teach about spiritual gifts because you have examined them for yourself, not just listened to someone else.[9] Ponder what the New Testament teaches. Prayerfully consider whether any of the gifts mentioned in the Bible are yours.

The pastoral epistles may also prove helpful. Reading Paul's exhortations to two church leaders, Titus and Timothy, I became convinced that I too had the gift of being a leader, perhaps even of being a pastor.

Prayer and Bible study are by far the most crucial and important steps to take in discovering your spiritual gifts. Don't disdain to use what God has made available. You cannot take a short cut around these two vital disciplines of the Christian life.

Contemplation. The third step of discovery is to sit back and reflect on those things you really enjoy doing, activities which repeatedly bring satisfaction. Think about your desires and inclinations. Paul

Little was fond of pointing out the misconception that God is an ogre who wants us to be miserable, wants us to go places we don't want to go, to do things we don't want to do.[10] But God's will is not normally to make us do what we hate more than anything else! As a rule, he has given us our likes and dislikes, our preferences and desires, for a purpose.

In his book *Knowing God's Will* Blaine Smith says that "God exercises his providence in creating our personalities. I may trust that he has not allowed my particular personality to develop by accident but has fashioned my inclinations and preferences as a means of motivating me in certain directions. By looking to the desires that are most basic to my personality, I can gain vital insights into where God is leading me."[11] In the same way I can gain insight into what spiritual gifts I have. Feelings and inclinations are not always dependable and may even be deceptive. Yet there are in all of us patterns of desire, motivation and inclination that God has placed there. Some are patterns that have been with us since childhood and will always be there. This is how God has made us . . . and re-made us! So consider those things you have enjoyed doing over the years. Consider what has given you the most satisfaction and fulfillment. Ponder those desires that are most basic to you as a person and individual.

Affirmation. The fourth step is to seek out the opinions of fellow Christians. Others often see us more clearly than we see ourselves. The writer of Proverbs has a few sharp-witted comments about this subject:

Listen to advice and accept instruction,
  and in the end you will be wise. (19:20)
Perfume and incense bring joy to the heart,
  and the pleasantness of one's friend springs
    from his earnest counsel. (27:9)

We need the affirmation of others who, like us, have the Spirit of God. In writing to the Corinthians, Paul gave his opinions regarding marriage and singleness. In 1 Corinthians 7:40 he suggests that the Christian widow in the Corinthian church would be happier if she remained a widow and did not seek to remarry. To give weight to his opinion he adds this comment: "And I think that I too have the Spirit of God." We need to listen to our spiritual leaders because they too are led by the Spirit. We do not have a corner on the Holy Spirit. While the opinions of other Christians do not automatically bind us, they are a valuable spiritual resource.

One day when my twin brother and I were both single, I realized that a Christian girl I knew might just be Jim's type. I encouraged him to ask her out, believing they would hit it off. They did, and now they're married with three children. I did this not because I'm a chronic matchmaker but because I wanted to throw the weight of my opinion behind the opinion my brother was already beginning to form. Later I sought out Jim's opinion when I met the person who turned out to be my wife. His opinion helped me have more confidence in mine.

Don't fall prey to the unhappy conviction that you alone are wise. Seldom do we see ourselves as others see us. Even more seldom do we see ourselves as we truly are. The opinions of people whose minds are enlightened by the Holy Spirit are worth listening to and should be taken into consideration. We all need the input that only our family, friends and church can give us.

Experimentation. Once you suspect you have a certain gift, the next step is simply to try it out.[12] Put it to work and see (1) if you enjoy using this gift, (2) if other people benefit from your use of this gift, and (3) if you feel comfortable and fulfilled exercising it. In brief, find out if this gift fits you. If it stems from the grace that God has given your unique self, then it will fit—it will correspond to the new you God has made.

Do you think you have the ability to lead? Seek an opportunity within your church or fellowship to lead in some capacity. Anything will do for starters. Do you think your gift is teaching? Find a way to do some teaching in your Christian education department. Don't be pushy; just offer your services, perhaps under a teacher who could nurture your gift.

If you suspect that one of your gifts is being merciful, get involved in a social ministry. See what local ministries are in place—neighborhood pantries or halfway houses. Try visiting the sick or elderly, or being a Big Brother to an orphan or handicapped child. Or simply make it a point to help fellow Christians who are in need.

If you think your gift is service, you might ask one of your deacons to include you in some of their activities so that you can get a taste of what they do. In doing this you can cultivate a sensitivity for the needs of others. Often, however, this fifth step of discovery manifests itself more by accident than by purpose.

Jim was a member of a small church that needed someone to lead the youth group. No one else volunteered, so Jim decided to give it a try. Much to his surprise, he enjoyed it. He fit. Because he cared enough to try, he learned that he had the gift. If you

don't accept challenges, you may not find out what
God has gifted you to do.[13]

Discovering the gifts God has entrusted to you is
a five-step process. It involves (1) praying, (2) study-
ing and meditating on Scripture, (3) thinking about
your most basic desires, (4) seeking the opinions of
others, and (5) using your suspected gifts.[14] Once
you become aware of your gifts, you can function as
a true servant in the church, and your Christian life
will be enriched as you enrich others. But now having *discovered* your gifts your lifelong task will be
to *develop* your gifts for more fruitful service.

Developing Your Spiritual Gifts

Have you ever known a church where it seems like
the pastor is doing all the work? He works eighty or
more hours a week, and the congregation is content
because, after all, that's what he's getting paid for?
But the people in such a church do not grow much.
They are not developing their spiritual gifts. Spiritual gifts only develop when they are put to work.
So here are five practical suggestions that should
help you become a better steward of your gifts.

Accept Responsibility

Accepting responsibility is like the fifth step of discovery, experimentation, in that you are purposely accepting a job which requires a gift. But the difference is you know what gift you have. Physical exercise develops muscles and builds stamina, and spiritual exercise will develop spiritual gifts, building confidence and a sense of self-worth. So look for a responsibility that will exercise your gift.

For a number of years Suzee did not realize she was gifted in relating to internationals. Then one day a Japanese family moved in up the street. Soon she became good friends with Samiko, the mother, and began helping her with English skills. Through Samiko she met Umeko, with whom she had a Bible study and shared the gospel. As time went by Suzee developed friendships with more internationals, some of whom were students at the local university. Today she is on staff with Inter-Varsity Christian Fellowship as an International Student specialist.

Almost by accident, Suzee discovered a spiritual gift she possessed. But having seen how God used her in an international relationship, she sought out more international friendships. Eventually Suzee developed her spiritual gift to the point where she felt led to make it a vocation. While not all of us make a vocation out of our spiritual gifts, Suzee's experience illustrates how each of us can be in the business of developing them.

If you are a Christian leader, a number one priority of your ministry should be to give people responsibilities in the areas in which they show gifts. In fact, the primary purpose of the Christian leader is "to prepare God's people for *works of service,* so that the body of Christ may be built up" (Eph 4:12). If you are not encouraging people to develop their gifts, you are not helping them grow as they should—and you are not doing your part in building the body of Christ as *you* should. So delegate responsibility, even if you'd "rather do it yourself." Make a list of jobs, functions and ministries presently done by the church's (or fellowship's) busiest people, and determine which ones can be delegated to others. After identifying different people's gifts, see that they all get some exercise.

If you are not a leader, ask for and accept tasks which fit in with your spiritual gifts. If your church or fellowship group is not yet active in the area in which you are gifted, you may have to create a new ministry. This is as it should be in the church. Gifts are given to complement each other, not to duplicate. God is a good and wise giver. Share your gifts and burdens with your leaders and see how they react. In most cases leaders are delighted to see initiative. And the whole church grows.

Seek Feedback

Another way to develop spiritual gifts is by seeking encouragement and feedback. This is like using the old Boy Scout buddy system. Each scout at the pool or waterfront pairs up with a friend, and these two become responsible for each other. Each is supposed to make sure that the other does not drown or get into trouble. Whenever the lifeguard blows his whistle and yells "Buddy check!" the boys have ten seconds to find their buddy and hold clasped hands over their heads.

Let a buddy help you develop your spiritual gifts. Find one or more friends you can confide in. Tell them about your gifts and responsibilities. Then ask them to observe your ministry and give you feedback and evaluation. Meet with them on a regular basis to receive this feedback. Ideally they will encourage more than criticize!

Many pastors, teachers and speakers have found this system helpful. Pastors have asked one or two people in the congregation to evaluate their sermons. These are not self-appointed critics but people the pastor has personally asked to serve this way. Their feedback helps him work harder on his weak-

nesses and lets him know what the people most
need to hear. It also helps him know when his ser-
mon is hitting home. The buddy system can help
you develop your gift as well.

Learn from Others

The Bible is full of examples of people who learned
from more experienced men and women of God. Consider the special Old Testament relationships between Joshua and Moses and between Elisha and
Elijah. These were disciples who attached themselves to one person and learned from him all they
could. In the New Testament we see the disciples
learning from Jesus, and Timothy learning from
Paul.

Look with me more closely at one other New Testament example: John Mark. Mark was determined
to learn more about how to be a missionary from an
experienced missionary. He went as a helper with
Paul and Barnabas on their first missionary journey
(Acts 13:4-5). But by the time they reached Pamphy-
lia, John Mark had had enough and volunteered to
return home (Acts 13:13). We hear no more of John
Mark until Paul asks Barnabas to accompany him on
his second missionary journey (Acts 15:36-37). Barnabas wants to take John Mark with them again in

order to give him a second chance. But Paul wants nothing to do with the quitter. In fact, "they had such a sharp disagreement that they parted company. Barnabas took Mark and sailed for Cyprus, but Paul chose Silas and . . . went through Syria and Cilicia" (Acts 15:39-41).

With Barnabas, Mark got another chance, and this time he learned to be a missionary. In later years even uncompromising Paul was able to say of John Mark, "Get Mark and bring him with you, because he is helpful to me in my ministry" (2 Tim 4:11). Mark had developed the gift of being a missionary by learning from the more experienced Barnabas.

Perhaps through such a relationship with another Christian God will develop one of your gifts. Be alert to such opportunities. Observing a more mature Christian who has a similar gift can lead you into more effective service.

Explore Possibilities

Do you need ideas for how to exercise or expand the use of your spiritual gift? Try taking inventory of present needs in your church or group. This can be a continuing tool to help you discover God's will for your gifts. Let's look at some of the possibilities for three specific gifts.

Obviously God has given many kinds of speaking gifts. What are some possibilities you could explore if you had one of them? Your list might look like this: delivering messages in your church or fellowship meetings, speaking at conferences or weekend retreats, leading a seminar, working at a Christian radio or television station, or teaching in any of several roles—as a Sunday-school teacher, a primary or secondary school teacher, a Christian college professor or a seminary instructor. Given thoughtfulness, imagination and verve you can come up with some exciting options.

If your gift is giving, it is even more important for you to take inventory. You need to consider all the possibilities available to you for financial involvement. Some categories you could list are your local church, your denomination, parachurch organizations, foreign missions, Christian education, Christian literature, urban ministry, prison ministry and various social ministries. Even the categories could create a very long list, not to mention the choices within each category. Christian organizations always lack funds. Many have plans that go unimplemented because funds are not available. This is why Christian giving plays such a vital role in ministry and service.

We need to decide carefully where to put our money and how much to give, whether giving is our particular gift or not. Charts can be of great help in organizing thoughts. Try making a chart, listing across the top some broad categories that you wish to support, and under each the particular ministries that are meeting needs in that category.

Having listed those ministries for which you feel concern, circle those you feel strongest about and place a dollar figure next to it. This is planned and purposeful giving, as opposed to haphazard or spontaneous giving. Instead of responding only to sporadic appeals, you can give thoughtfully and strategically. Christian ministries benefit more from regular, consistent contributions they can count on than from sporadic or one-time giving. Planned giving allows you to easily review your priorities as God lays new burdens on your heart. And the chart will remind you of long-term commitments as well.

But perhaps your gift is hospitality. What are some possibilities here? You can plan to entertain church families or teen-agers. You could host game nights or other social activities. You could regularly invite in your neighbors, possibly sharing the gospel with them. You could host international students, elderly people, unwanted or disabled children, unwed mothers-to-be or disturbed teens. Opening your house to non-Christians can be a tremendous way to expose them to a Christian environment and atmosphere. As with the gift of giving, make a list or chart of all the ideas you can come up with. It's a good way to confirm that you're using your gift in meaningful ways.

Whatever gift you have, first inventory your own church or fellowship, and then move on to other areas. As the years go by, your basic gifts will probably remain the same (Rom 11:29), but there will be wide latitude for growth and application. Explore the possibilities; push beyond the boundaries of what you've done so far. As you do, your gifts will develop.

Plan Your Life

Gifts may be continually encouraged by planned and purposeful living. About a year ago my church began having a "children's focus" during morning worship. It was designed to be a five-minute talk or story which taught a spiritual truth to the small children of our congregation. It was set up on a volunteer basis. Since volunteers were not rushing forward, I felt that I should help out occasionally, even though I have never felt gifted in ministry to children. After

my third or fourth attempt at this, I was firmly convinced that my gifts did not lie in this area. And my
friends enthusiastically agreed.

We all learn some lessons in the school of hard
knocks. But if we plan for the using of our gifts,
these hard-learned lessons can be fewer. We need to
learn to be selective about which jobs we accept.
People who say yes to everything are not only being
unfair to themselves and others, but they may also
be taking time and energy away from another ministry they ought to be doing. Don't spread yourself
too thin! God has given us complementary gifts so
that none of us can or should do it all. The Giver of
gifts will orchestrate the whole body so that we each
are free to concentrate on our own small part and do
it well.

To plan your life, list your gifts as you and others
see them. Now, opposite each gift, jot down some
possible ministries, responsibilities or applications.
Think about things you have done well in the past.
Put an asterisk beside each activity you would espe-
cially like to see yourself doing. You will not be
foresighted enough to include all future possibilities, but at least you will have a list of *some* things
you are capable of doing and will know which way
you'd like to grow. More important, you will have a

permanent record of your gifts.

If you live in such a planned and purposeful way for the next few months and then the next few years, you will develop a firm pattern in your habits and in your thinking which corresponds closely to your gifts. Gradually you will be able to make future decisions more easily and confidently.

Jesus calls his disciples to a lifetime of service. By his example he has shown the way of grace: "Whoever wants to become great among you must be your servant, and whoever wants to be first must be slave of all" (Mk 10:43-44). You manifest the grace of God in your life when you employ your spiritual gifts to serve others. Know them. Use them for the Lord.

Become aware of the spiritual gifts you already have so that you will be able to use them more effectively and strategically. Pray. Meditate on Scripture. Contemplate your most basic joys and desires. Seek out the opinions of fellow Christians. Then put your suspected gifts to work in actual ministry.

Once you have discovered one of your gifts, spend the rest of your life developing it. Accept responsibility in the area of your gift. Seek encouragement and feedback from trusted friends and leaders. Take inventory of the opportunities available for using your gifts. Learn from those who are more experienced. Plan your life; live purposefully. Strive to be one to whom Jesus says at the end of time, "Well done, good and faithful servant! You have been faithful with a few things; I will put you in charge of many things. Come and share your master's happiness!" (Mt 25:21).

Notes

[1]Also see Galatians 5:13-14.

[2]See the following on God's grace as enabling power: Lk 2:40; Acts 13:43; Rom 12:3; 2 Cor 1:12; 4:15; 6:1; 8:1-2; 9:14; 2 Tim 2:1; 1 Pet 4:10; Jn 1:14, 16; Acts 11:23; Rom 15:15-16; Eph 3:7; Heb 13:9.

[3]The Greek word rendered "according to" in Romans 12:6 may also be translated in three other ways: "corresponding to," "with reference to" and "just as."

[4]J. R. W. Stott, *Baptism and Fullness* (Downers Grove, Ill.: InterVarsity Press, 1975), pp. 89-90. Also see Eph 4:7-8.

[5]Examples of those who agree with this thesis are Stott, *Baptism and Fullness,* pp. 88-90; Charles E. Hummel, *Filled with the Spirit* (Downers Grove, Ill.: InterVarsity Press, 1981), pp. 18-19; C. Peter Wagner, *Your Spiritual Gifts Can Help Your Church Grow* (Ventura, Calif.: Ventura Books, 1979), pp. 62-63.

[6]Stott, *Baptism and Fullness,* p. 89; Walter Bauer, *A Greek-English Lexicon of the New Testament,* trans. W. F. Arndt and F. W. Gingrich (Chicago: Univ. of Chicago

Press, 1974), pp. 183, 622, 713-14.

[7]For ideas on what some of the gifts listed in the New Testament may refer to, see the following: Leslie B. Flynn, *19 Gifts of the Spirit* (Wheaton: Victor Books, 1975); Charles C. Ryrie, *The Holy Spirit* (Chicago: Moody Press, 1974), chap. 15; Bridge and Phypers, *Spiritual Gifts and the Church* (Downers Grove, Ill.: InterVarsity Press, 1973), chap. 4; Wagner, *Your Spiritual Gifts*, pp. 9, 259-63.

[8]G. C. Berkouwer, *Man: The Image of God* (Grand Rapids: Eerdmans, 1975), chaps. 3 & 6; Earl D. Wilson, *The Undivided Self* (Downers Grove, Ill.: InterVarsity Press, 1983).

[9]Following are all the occurrences of *dorea* in the New Testament: Jn 4:10; Acts 2:38; 8:20; 10:45; 11:17; Rom 5:15, 17; 1 Cor 9:15; Eph 3:7; 4:7; Heb 6:4. Following are all the uses of *pneumatikos* in the New Testament when it refers to spiritual gifts: Rom 1:11; 1 Cor 12:1; 14:1; 37. The occurrences of *charisma* in the New Testament are as follows: Rom 1:11; 5:15-16; 6:23; 11:29; 12:6; 1 Cor 1:7; 7:7; 12:4-6, 9, 28, 30-31; 2 Cor 1:11; 1 Tim 4:14; 2 Tim 1:6; 1 Pet 4:10.

[10]Paul Little, *Affirming the Will of God* (Downers Grove, Ill.: InterVarsity Press, 1971), pp. 11-12.

[1]M. Blaine Smith, *Knowing God's Will* (Downers Grove, Ill.: InterVarsity Press, 1979), p. 89.

[2]Ibid., pp. 99-103.

[3]Ibid., p. 89.

[4]Wagner, *Your Spiritual Gifts*, on pages 116-33, outlines

five steps of discovery which are similar to the five steps I have presented. You may find them helpful: (1) explore the possibilities; (2) experiment with as many as you can; (3) examine your feelings; (4) evaluate your effectiveness; and (5) expect confirmation from the Body.

J. E. O'Day is a campus staff worker with Inter-Varsity Christian Fellowship in Bloomsburg, Pennsylvania.